Magical
POOPY
SURPRISE

SLIME SAFETY

- The activities in this book require adult supervision at all times.

- Ingredients may cause skin irritation – we recommend that gloves are worn when making or handling slime and that slime is not handled for prolonged periods of time.

- Always wash your hands and tools with soap and water and disinfect surfaces once you have finished an activity.

- Never eat or taste slime or slime-making ingredients.

- Make sure that slime is kept away from very young children and pets.

- Slime may stain – wear old clothes and cover surfaces to prevent damage.

- If any slime or slime-making ingredients come into contact with your eyes, flush well with water.

- Dispose of slime in a waste container in the dustbin – do not put slime down sinks or drains.

- Slime only has a short shelf life, throw away at the first sign of any mould or odour.

- The publisher shall not be liable or responsible in any respect for any use or application of any information or material contained in this book or any adverse effect, consequence, injury, loss or damage of any type resulting or arising from, directly or indirectly, the use or application of any information or material contained in this book.

Scholastic Children's Books,
Euston House, 24 Eversholt Street,
London NW1 1DB, UK

A division of Scholastic Ltd
London ~ New York ~ Toronto ~ Sydney ~ Auckland
Mexico City ~ New Delhi ~ Hong Kong

Published in the UK by Scholastic Ltd, 2019
Produced by Cloud King Creative

ISBN 978 1407 1 9578 0

Printed in the UK by Bell and Bain Ltd, Glasgow

2 4 6 8 10 9 7 5 3

Papers used by Scholastic Children's Books are made from
wood grown in sustainable forests.

www.scholastic.co.uk

Magical POOPY SURPRISE

SCHOLASTIC

CONTENTS

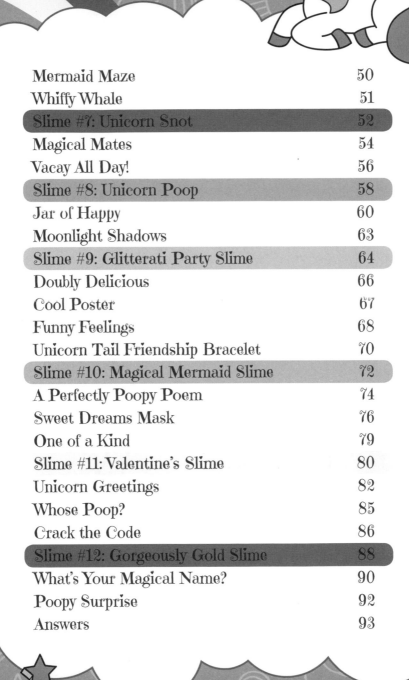

WELCOME!

... to a wonderful world where unicorns rock, narwhals rule and even the poops are magical!

Colour in this legend using the little picture as a guide.

This book is packed full of awesome activities, quirky quizzes, cute crafts ... plus some poopy surprises, too! Grab your pens and pencils and join in the super-pooper fun!

Meet Glitter Poop! He's hiding on five different pages throughout this book. Make a note of the pages where you found him below.

25 31 82

TIME TO GOO!

Squishy, stretchy and sometimes even poopy, with a little unicorn magic, making slime is easy! Read ingredients labels and follow the recipes carefully and you should be able to make magical mixtures in minutes. The slimes in this book can be made using ingredients found at home, in supermarkets, craft shops or online. Always shop online with an adult who can order for you.

A SLIMY SHOPPING LIST

The Base
Clear or white PVA glue (sometimes called 'school glue'). Clear glue requires less activator than white glue. Whichever type you use should be non-toxic, washable and list PVA (polyvinyl acetate) among its ingredients.

Remember!
Always have an adult around when you make or play with slime.

ACTIVATORS

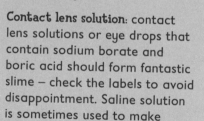

Contact lens solution: contact lens solutions or eye drops that contain sodium borate and boric acid should form fantastic slime – check the labels to avoid disappointment. Saline solution is sometimes used to make slime, too.

Bicarbonate of soda: this baking ingredient is added in small amounts to thicken the slime.

It can be used with or without contact lens solution as an activator.

Shaving foam: choose foam rather than shaving gel to create fluffy slime.

Liquid laundry detergent: choose a detergent that has boric acid listed in its ingredients.

EXTRAS

Paints: use acrylic paints to brighten up your slimes. Colour-changing iridescent shades are dazzling!

Food colouring (liquid or gel): gels often produce brighter, deeper colours than liquid food colouring and are less messy.

Glitter: normal or iridescent glitters give your slime an instant upgrade. Biodegradable glitters are best.

Sequins: different shapes, sizes and colours add shimmer and texture!

Beads: adding plastic or glass beads turns ordinary slime into noisy, crackling slime.

Baby oil or coconut oil: a drop of either oil will make your slime less sticky.

Lotion: baby lotion or unfragranced body lotion will make your slime stretchy.

Fragrance oil or handwash: use skin-safe oils that are suitable for making candles or soap. Handwash is a handy ingredient, too!

Kitchen roll: to wipe up mess and spills.

Chopping boards: useful for kneading slime on. Plastic ones are dishwasher safe and less likely to stain.

Mixing bowls: use a larger bowl when making fluffy slimes or larger batches.

Mixing utensils: spoons, spatulas or craft sticks are all great for mixing.

SIMPLE STEPS TO STAY SAFE WHILE MAKING SLIME:

* None of the slime recipes in this book are edible, so NEVER EAT slime at any time.
* Wash your hands well with soap before and after making slime.
* Always keep slime away from pets and very young children.
* Choose paints, glues and other ingredients that are non-toxic and washable.
* Clean any work surfaces before and after making slime.
* If your skin is sensitive, wear protective gloves whenever you touch slime or slime ingredients.
* Keep slime away from all carpets, sofas and other soft materials – wearing old clothes would be wise!
* Throw away any used slime in an old container or bag in the dustbin – never put slime down sinks or drains.

PONGY PATH

Make your way through this magical maze, avoiding five rainbow poops along the path.

Start

Finish

Answer is on page 93.

POOPY PATTERNS

Draw doodles on these doo-doos, then add some colour to make the poops look perfect!

HOW MAGICAL ARE YOU?

Magic is all around us, you just have to know where to look. But exactly how magical are you? Extremely enchanting or as normal as night follows day?

1. How long have you believed in magic?

A. My whole life! ☐
B. Many magical years! ☐
C. I'm not sure magic is real. ☐

2. Circle the poop that makes you feel the most magical!

A

B.

C.

3. Where do narwhals live?

A. They splash about in my dreams! ☐
B. In places where mermaids also swim. ☐
C. In the sparkling Arctic Ocean. ☐

4. Circle the accessory that gives you added sparkle!

A.

B.

C.

5. What colour would you paint your dream bedroom?

A. Rainbow, of course! ☐
B. The perfect shade of pink. ☐
C. A cool grey works for me. ☐

6. What kind of dreams do you have?

A. Wonderful ones set in magical worlds! ☐
B. Ordinary ones about things that happen in real life. ☐
C. I can never remember my dreams in the morning. ☐

Mostly As

Merlin's beard! In touch with your inner unicorn, you're as magical as they come.

Mostly Bs

Your heart and mind are full of magic – never lose your sparkle.

Mostly Cs

You're yet to discover the magic inside of you – let your imagination fly!

SUPER FLUFFY SLIME

Supersize your slime by adding shaving foam – it will make your mix super fluffy and as soft as a cloud!

What you'll need:

- 500 ml white or clear PVA glue
- 125 ml shaving foam
- food colouring or acrylic paint
- liquid laundry detergent

Tip to Try! Storing slime in an airtight container will make it last longer. Reuse packaging if you can.

1 Pour the glue into a large mixing bowl. Add the shaving foam, gently folding it into the glue.

FANTASTIC

2

Choose the colour you'd like your slime to be, then add some food colouring or paint. Fold in gently until the mixture has completely combined.

3

Add laundry detergent, a drop at a time, and mix well. The mixture should begin to come away from the sides of the bowl.

4

Gently knead the slime on a clean work surface until it reaches a slime consistency. Be careful not to work the slime too hard.

FLUFFY STUFF!

FANTASTIC FRIENDS CROSSWORD

Fill in the crossword using the clues to help you. Each answer is a magical creature!

DOWN

1. Half human, half fish, this singing siren is said to live out at sea.

2. A winged unicorn that has the freedom of the skies.

6. A mash-up of an eagle and a lion!

ACROSS

3. A tiny, magical being with a human appearance.

4. A flying horse from Greek mythology.

5. Scaly creatures, some species can breathe flames.

7. The most famous fabled creature with a magical horn.

8. A legendary bird that can be reborn out of fire.

CLUES

Use a mirror if you get stuck! Choose from:

Alicorn, dragon, fairy, griffin, mermaid, Pegasus, phoenix, unicorn.

1

2

3 ◯◯◯◯◯

4 ◯◯◯◯ A ◯◯◯

5 ◯◯◯◯ 6G ◯◯◯

7 ◯◯◯◯◯◯◯◯

8P ◯◯◯◯◯◯

Answers are on page 93.

POOP THE RAINBOW!

These cute creatures go crazy for rainbow colours! Circle twelve differences in the picture on the opposite page.

Colour in a unicorn poop for each
difference you find.

MAGICAL RAINBOW SLIME

Super-colourful and squishy, this slime combines all the colours of the rainbow! Adding glitter will make your slime more magical still!

What you'll need:

- 1 large batch of fluffy slime
- food colouring or paint for each rainbow colour
- 7 small containers
- glitter (optional)

Tip to Try!
Take care not to overmix the colours, or your slime may go brown.

1

Start by making a large batch of white fluffy slime (the recipe is on pages 16–17).

Washing your hands after kneading each batch will stop the colours from transferring.

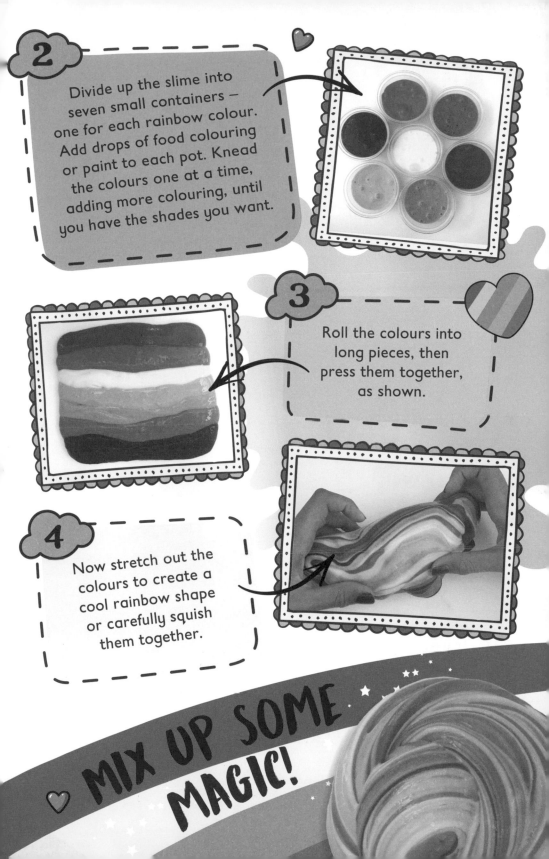

2 Divide up the slime into seven small containers — one for each rainbow colour. Add drops of food colouring or paint to each pot. Knead the colours one at a time, adding more colouring, until you have the shades you want.

3 Roll the colours into long pieces, then press them together, as shown.

4 Now stretch out the colours to create a cool rainbow shape or carefully squish them together.

♡ MIX UP SOME MAGIC!

WOULD YOU RATHER...

Answer these tough teasers alone or with your best friend – for added giggles!

	Me	BFF
Brush your hair with a cactus	☐	☐
or		
step in unicorn poop?	☐	☐
Have a best friend who's a mermaid	☐	☐
or		
a unicorn as a pet?	☐	☐
Be able to fly like an alicorn	☐	☐
or		
gallop like a unicorn?	☐	☐
Have magical powers	☐	☐
or		
super powers?	☐	☐
Be given a new pair of shoes every week	☐	☐
or		
a new hat twice a week?	☐	☐
Be a prize-winning artist	☐	☐
or		
an extraordinary explorer?	☐	☐

	Me	BFF
Meet your favourite celebrity	☐	☐
or		
appear in your favourite TV show?	☐	☐
Live in the future	☐	☐
or		
live in the past?	☐	☐
Dye your hair rainbow colours	☐	☐
or		
grow a rainbow-coloured beard?	☐	☐
Live in a cabin in the mountains	☐	☐
or		
a beach hut by the ocean?	☐	☐
Have the voice of a mermaid	☐	☐
or		
the healing powers of a unicorn?	☐	☐
Have a house with trampoline floors	☐	☐
or		
an aquarium in your basement?	☐	☐
Be a unicorn for an hour	☐	☐
or		
be a sloth for a day?	☐	☐

FRIENDLY FACES

Copy and colour the other half of each friendly face. Give each cutie a name and scribble down something it loves!

Name:
....
....

Loves:
....
....

Name:
....
....

Loves:
....
....

Name:

Loves:

Name:

Loves:

27

DREAMY ICE-CREAM SLIME

We all scream for ice cream ... slime!
Remember though, while this sweet treat
looks delish it's definitely not edible!

What you'll need:

- 250 ml white PVA glue
- 60 ml shaving foam
- liquid laundry detergent
- pink food colouring
- hundreds and thousands

Tip to Try!
Work in a few drops
of activator at a time
until the slime no
longer sticks to your
fingers.

1

Pour the glue into a
bowl. Add the shaving
foam, folding it gently
into the glue.

A TRULY COOL

2

Next, add drops of laundry detergent, mixing as you go, until you have a fluffy slime consistency.

3

Fold in drops of food colouring until your mixture is the perfect shade of pink, then knead the slime with your hands.

4

Sprinkle hundreds and thousands of hundreds and thousands into the slime!

SLIME

HAPPY HAIR-DOO

This unfortunate unicorn has lost her sparkle! Doodle patterns and add colour to give her a magical makeover.

MAGICAL MEMORY GAME

Is your memory as sharp as a unicorn's horn or as squishy as a unicorn poop? Try this activity to see!

Study the pictures on this page for sixty seconds, and then turn over to the next page and draw everything you can remember.

QUICK DRAW!

How many unicorn goodies can you remember?
Draw or write down as many things as you can –
without peeking!

When you're ready, turn to the previous page to check the answers. Then work out your score!

How did you score?

1-3 Your head is in the clouds! Try again to draw what you saw.

4-6 Not bad, but your brain could do with a boost.

7-9 Nailed it! Your memory rocks.

All 10 You're a quiz whizz with a magical memory!

SAY WHAT?

The names of these magical creatures have been mysteriously scrambled! Grab a timer, then try to work out their real names in less than two minutes.

1 COINRUN

_ _ _ _ _ _ _

2 FRIFING

_ _ _ _ _ _ _

3 EARDIMM

_ _ _ _ _ _ _

4 PIXHONE

_ _ _ _ _ _ _

5 GRODNA

_ _ _ _ _ _

6 RAILNCO

_ _ _ _ _ _ _

MY TIME:

_ _ : _ _

Answers are on page 93.

HOW TO DRAW A UNICORN

Follow these five steps to draw
a super-cute unicorn!

CRUNCHY FOAM SLIME

Mix in foam balls to give your fluffy slime some crunch. Make a big batch to share with other slime fans!

What you'll need:

- 500 ml white PVA glue
- 120 ml shaving foam
- liquid laundry detergent
- small coloured foam balls

Tip to Try!
Dispose of your slime in the dustbin if it starts to smell or change colour.

1 Pour the glue into a bowl. Add a couple of squirts of shaving foam and fold it gently into the glue.

GIVE THIS A

2 Add a small amount of laundry detergent and mix well. Add more detergent to activate the slime, as needed.

3 Knead the mixture until it turns into a slime consistency.

4 Add the foam balls and fold the mixture with your hands until everything has combined. Simple!

SQUASH

UNICORN POOP TREATS

Made with just four ingredients and ready in under an hour, these no-bake unicorn poop treats are so easy to make and healthy, too!

What you'll need:

 125 g coconut flour

350 g smooth cashew butter*

85 g maple syrup

1–2 tbsp hundreds and thousands

*Important allergy advice: nut allergy sufferers should replace the cashew butter with sunflower seed butter or biscuit spread.

1
Line a baking tray or chopping board with greaseproof paper and put to one side.

2
Sieve the coconut flour into a large mixing bowl. Add your cashew butter and maple syrup and mix until combined.

3

Next, stir in the hundreds and thousands. If the mixture is too thin, stir in more coconut flour, a spoonful at a time. If the mixture is too thick, add a little milk or water.

4

Using your hands, form small balls. Roll each ball into a sausage shape and make a point at one end.

5

Make each sausage into a poopy pile shape with the point at the top and place on the greaseproof paper.

6

Place the tray in the fridge for at least thirty minutes, or until the treats have firmed up.

YUM!

PRETTY POMPOM SLIME

Give clear slime texture by adding pompoms in cool colours for a slime that's satisfying to stretch and squish!

What you'll need:

- 125 ml clear PVA glue
- 30 ml water
- 1/2 tsp bicarbonate of soda
- contact lens solution
- pompoms (different colours and sizes work well)

1

Pour the glue and water into a bowl and mix.

TOTALLY ON TREND!

2
Add the bicarbonate of soda and stir until it has dissolved.

3
Next, add the contact lens solution, one squirt at a time. Mix well and knead until the slime is the right consistency.

4
Toss in your pompoms, folding them into the mixture with your hands.

BEASTLY BUDDIES QUIZ

Can't make up your mind about which animal to adopt? Answer the questions in this quiz to decide what would be the perfect pet for you!

START

Do you need your pet to be cute and fluffy?

NO

YES

Would your friends describe you as crazy and colourful?

YES

NO

Do you favour adventures abroad over staycations?

NO

Is your favourite place to chill out the sofa?

YES

Do you want a party animal for a pet?

YES

NO

YES

Narwhals... too cute for words?

YES

Would you like your pet to be able to take you for a ride?

YES

Would you prefer a pet whose poop is magical?

YES

NO

NO

NO

NO

YES

Would you prefer an affectionate pet?

YES

NO

Do you own any balls of wool?

YES

Unique unicorn
Why not get a pet that will stand out from the crowd? A unicorn is as individual as you are and — like you — cannot be tamed!

Llam-azing llama
Your ideal animal is tons of fun! Bright-eyed and confident, it could carry your shopping home, too.

Cute kitty
Your purr-fect pet is a furry feline! Just like you, your pet is lovable but independent.

43

POOPY PUNS CHALLENGE

Take on a friend to see who can keep a straight face the longest – players mustn't laugh, snigger or even smile. It's the only game where laughter is for losers!

Q: What do you call an exploding unicorn?
A: Pop-corn!

Q: What do you call a pooping fairy?
A: Stinkerbell!

Q: Why did the unicorn cross the road?
A: Because somebody shouted "hay"!

Q: When will a unicorn say hello?
A: Whinny wants to!

Q: Why did the toilet paper roll down the hill?
A: It wanted to get to the bottom!

Q: What is brown and sticky?
A: A stick!

What to do:

- Sit across from each other and take it in turns to read out the jokes below.
- Pulling funny faces and making silly sound effects are allowed, too!
- If you make your opponent laugh or smile, you win a point.
- If your opponent doesn't laugh or smile, they win a point.
- The first person to win three points wins the game!

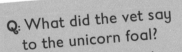
PLAYER 2 JOKES

Q: What did the unicorn say when it fell over?
A: "Help! I can't giddy-up!"

Q: What did one toilet say to the other toilet?
A: "You look flushed!"

Q: Why did the unicorn bring toilet paper to the party?
A: Because he was a party pooper.

Q: What looks like half a unicorn?
A: The other half!

Q: What did the vet say to the unicorn foal?
A: You're just a little horse.

Q: What's poopy and sounds like a bell?
A: Dung!

SWEET SCENTED SLIME

Spark your sense of smell
by adding a sweet scent to your slime!
Choose from cola, bubblegum, chocolate
or mix in your own fave fragrance!

What you'll need:

- 100 ml white PVA glue
- 1/4 tsp bicarbonate of soda
- contact lens solution
- scented liquid handwash

1

Pour the white glue into a bowl.

2

Mix together the bicarbonate of soda, with squirts of contact lens solution until you have a slime consistency.

3

Add some handwash (chocolate orange smells scrummy!), one squirt at a time, and mix well. The slime should become smooth and glossy.

4

When the slime is ready, remove it from the bowl. Sniff it, stretch it and let it slide through your fingers!

Tip to Try!
Skin-safe fragrance oils or candle scents can be used instead of handwash, while food colouring will brighten up your slime.

SMELLS SO SWEET!

SURPRISING SELFIES

Fill these pages with pics of you and your BFFs that capture your LOL moments! You could add captions, too.

MERMAID MAZE

Help Marina the mermaid find her magical lost treasure. It's somewhere under the sea! Swim past five friendly turtles on your way.

Answer is on page 93.

WHIFFY WHALE

Starting at number 1, join the dots to reveal
a unicorn of the sea.

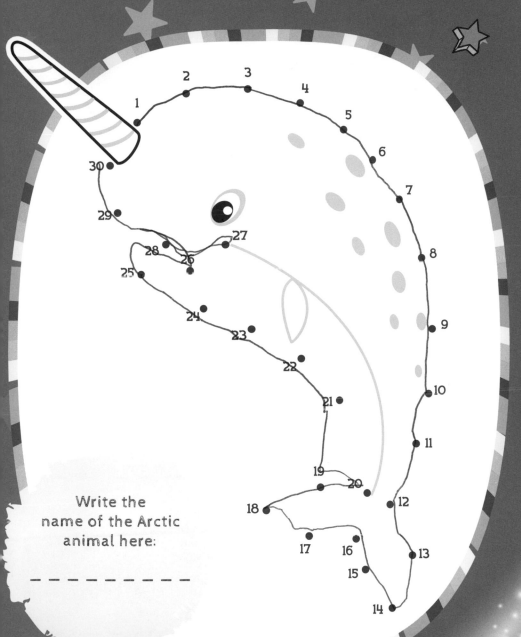

Write the
name of the Arctic
animal here:

_ _ _ _ _ _ _ _

UNICORN SNOT

'Snot as gross as it sounds, this super-stretchy slime is the pick of the bunch!

What you'll need:

- 125 ml clear PVA glue
- 30 ml water
- 1/2 tsp bicarbonate of soda
- bright green paint
- contact lens solution

1 Add the glue to a bowl.

2 Pour in the water and mix well.

2

Stir in the bicarbonate of soda, which will thicken the slime.

3

Pour in enough paint to make the mixture turn bright green.

4

Mix in squirts of contact lens solution until the slime pulls away easily from sides of the bowl.

Tip to Try!
Using a tape measure, see how far you can stretch this slime.

A GOO THAT'S EEWWW!

MAGICAL MATES

Draw doodles in the clouds or stick
in selfies to decide which of your friends
best suits each caption.

My funniest friend: ....

My kindest friend: ....

My loudest friend:

My most stylish friend:

My most magical friend:

MY BFFS!

My cheekiest friend:

55

VACAY ALL DAY!

Because even unicorns need time off! Search for ten holiday words in the word search on the opposite page. The words read forwards, down and diagonally.

selfie

city

pool

ice cream

inflatable

suitcase

relax

sandcastle

hotel

explore

```
t  w  h  o  t  e  l  f  v  b  c  c  q  a
p  s  c  v  s  r  e  l  a  x  f  i  i  p
d  e  y  m  a  c  v  t  z  i  y  s  t  t
a  l  h  n  p  g  i  p  d  p  c  u  b  y
g  f  s  g  t  h  c  b  n  o  q  i  p  j
k  i  k  n  v  d  e  y  e  o  a  t  k  e
t  e  b  t  b  x  c  s  q  l  d  c  f  x
h  p  d  a  q  j  r  a  x  p  n  a  v  p
q  t  g  y  r  n  e  p  z  r  k  s  w  l
f  s  i  n  f  l  a  t  a  b  l  e  y  o
a  k  c  s  w  g  m  h  b  h  s  v  h  r
s  a  n  d  c  a  s  t  l  e  w  c  g  e
w  y  b  j  v  k  j  v  g  k  r  f  q  j
c  r  h  w  a  f  w  s  m  t  h  t  o  i
```

Find five letters in bold and write them below. Then unscramble them to reveal the unicorns' #1 vacay hangout!

_____ _____ _____ _____ _____

Answers are on page 93.

UNICORN POOP

Fantastically fluffy, this pretty poop is the stuff of legends! When you gotta goo, you gotta goo!

What you'll need:

- large batch of fluffy slime (see pages 16-17)
- purple, pink and pearl-white iridescent paints
- 3 bowls or containers
- glitter or sequins (optional)

Tip to Try!
Place any hard or dry slime in a bowl of warm water, then stretch it out.

1

Divide a large batch of fluffy white slime into three equal parts. Using a clean bowl for each colour, squirt in paint and mix until you have the shade you want. Knead the coloured slimes, one at a time.

Washing your hands after kneading each batch will stop the colours from transferring.

2

Roll the colours into sausage-like pieces and gently press them together.

3

Stretch and twist your slime, taking care not to mix the colours completely.

4

Shake on some extra glitter or sequins to give your slime a magical shimmer!

POOP-TASTIC!

JAR OF HAPPY

Have you ever wanted to be as happy as a unicorn? Make your own Jar of Happy and pick a different note to bring a smile to your face each day!

What you'll need:

 a large jar with a lid

 ribbon or stickers to decorate your jar

 scissors

1 Choose a jar that's large enough to hold your happiness notes.

2 Ask an adult to help you cut out the notes on the opposite page.

3 Fold the notes and pop them in the jar.

4 Add more notes over time – why not write down things that make you happy?

5   Take a note from the jar and read whenever you need a little sparkle in your life!

If at first you don't succeed, click your heels and try again.

In a field full of horses, be a unicorn.

Why fit in when you were born to stand out?

Happiness is a unicorn pooping rainbows.

Do the right thing, even when no one's watching.

Dream big.

You are 99% unicorn.

Be honest. Be kind. Be magical.

Make a wish.

You are somebody's reason to smile.

Believe in magic and you will find it.

Reach for the stars!

Paint the town rainbow.

May all your dreams come true.

Party like a unicorn.

You are smart. You are strong. You can do anything.

Always be yourself, unless you can be a unicorn.

Believe in your inner unicorn.

You are magical.

You don't need wings to fly.

You're one of a kind, born to be wild.

Anything is possible.

Whatever you do, have fun.

Make your own magic.

Never stop dreaming.

You can't have a rainbow without a little rain.

It's going to be a rainbow and unicorns kind of day.

Time spent playing is never time wasted.

Unicorns can't fly. You can't fly... You are a unicorn!

A smile is the best make-up.

Dreams are the playground of unicorns.

You are like a unicorn: rare, sweet and magical.

MOONLIGHT SHADOWS

After dark is when unicorns look their most magical! Draw lines to match each unicorn to the shadow it has cast.

Answers are on page 93.

GLITTERATI PARTY SLIME

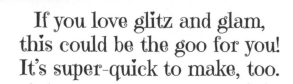

If you love glitz and glam,
this could be the goo for you!
It's super-quick to make, too.

What you'll need:

- 125 ml clear PVA glue or glitter glue
- 30 ml water
- 1/2 tsp bicarbonate of soda
- contact lens solution
- glitter – iridescent ones are so sparkly!

1

Pour the glue and water into a bowl and mix. You can skip step 3 if you use glitter glue!

2

Add the bicarbonate of soda and mix until it has dissolved.

3

Choose your favourite shade of glitter, or mix in two colours together for extra sparkle.

4

Next, add squirts of contact lens solution, mixing as you go.

5

Stretch and knead your glitter slime until it is the perfect consistency.

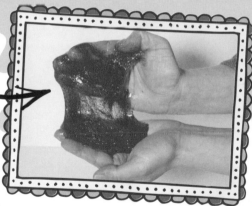

PERFECT FOR PARTIES!

Tip to Try!
Add acrylic paint or food colouring to give your slime a splash of colour!

DOUBLY DELICIOUS

Circle the two cupcakes that are exactly the same among this delightful dozen.

Answer is on page 93.

♡ FUNNY FEELINGS

Work out the current mood of each unicorn
by matching the words to the emojis.

1 surprised

2 thoughtful

3 in love

4 puzzled

5 grumpy

6 super happy

7 kinda sad

8 freaked out

#MANYMOODS

UNICORN TAIL FRIENDSHIP BRACELET

The magic of friendship ties everyone together! Make these special friendship bracelets with your friends at your next sleepover.

What you'll need:

- ♥ embroidery threads
- ♥ scissors
- ♥ sticky tape

1. Cut the threads to the same length as from your shoulder to your fingertips.

2. Tie them together in a knot. Tape the end to a flat surface.

3. Knot the far-left thread (blue) to the next thread along (yellow), by taking the left thread over the top of the second thread. Pull until the knot moves up to the top of the yellow thread. Pull it tight. Repeat, tying the blue over the yellow again.

4. Tie the first (blue) thread around the third (pink) thread. Pull tight to the top in a knot. Do this one more time.

5. Repeat steps 3 and 4, knotting the left-hand thread to the middle thread twice and then to the right-hand thread twice.

6. Continue knotting the far-left thread around the other threads from left to right.

7. Keep going until the bracelet is long enough to fit your friend's wrist.

8. Tie a knot in the end and trim any excess thread. Tie the bracelet on to your friend's wrist!

SUPER CUTE!

Now help your buddy make a matching bracelet for you!

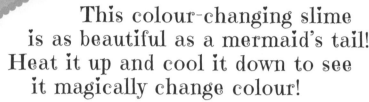

MAGICAL MERMAID SLIME

This colour-changing slime
is as beautiful as a mermaid's tail!
Heat it up and cool it down to see
it magically change colour!

What you'll need:

* 125 ml clear PVA glue
* 1/4 tsp bicarbonate of soda
* 1 tbsp liquid laundry detergent
* acrylic paint
* 1/4 tsp colour-changing nail pigment powder

1 Pour the glue into a mixing bowl.

2 Add the bicarbonate of soda. Mix until it dissolves.

3 Next, add a squirt of laundry detergent and mix in some acrylic paint.

4 Once the mixture starts to come together, add the nail pigment powder. Knead the slime with your hands until it's no longer sticky.

5 Warm your hands, then press down on the slime for incredible results!

COLOURS CHANGE BEFORE YOUR EYES!

Tip to Try!
Dip the slime into a bowl of iced water, or heat it with a hairdryer to reveal different shades.

A PERFECTLY POOPY POEM

An acrostic poem is a fun poem in which the first letters of each line spell out a word or phrase. The poem doesn't need to rhyme and the lines can be a single word or a whole sentence – it's up to you!

Sometimes
Unicorn
Rainbow
Poop
Really
Isn't
So
Epic!

S
U
R
P
R
I
S
E

Now choose any word you like and write a second poem. You could spell out your name or a friend's.

SWEET DREAMS MASK

Make this special sleep mask to slip on when you need a nap ... because even unicorns need their beauty sleep!

What you'll need:

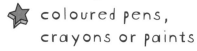
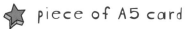

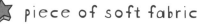

- coloured pens, crayons or paints
- piece of A5 card
- piece of wadding
- piece of soft fabric
- length of elastic (about 40 cm)
- glitter and glue (or glitter glue)
- scissors

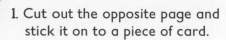

1. Cut out the opposite page and stick it on to a piece of card.

2. Glue the wadding on to the reverse of the page within the mask outline.

3. Glue a soft piece of fabric on top of the wadding and leave to dry.

4. Carefully cut out the mask shape. Ask an adult to help – you may need sharp scissors.

5. Colour your sleep mask in magical colours. Glitter will really make your mask sparkle!

6. Ask an adult to make holes on either side of the mask.

7. Measure a piece of elastic that will fit your head size. Put a large knot in one end, then thread it through one of the holes at the front of the mask Feed the other end through the hole and make another knot on the opposite side.

PUT ON YOUR MASK, READY TO CATCH SOME ZZZZS!

#FEELINGPOOPED

ONE OF A KIND

One of these unicorns is different from his brothers in the blessing. Place a tick next to the odd unicorn out.

VALENTINE'S SLIME

Surprise someone you admire
with this romantic glitter slime.
What's not to love?

What you'll need:

* 125 ml clear PVA glue
* 30 ml water
* 1/4 tsp bicarbonate of soda
* contact lens solution
* red or pink glitter
* love heart sequins

Tip to Try!
Add a little hot water
or baby oil if your
slime begins to
break apart.

1

Pour the glue
and water into
a bowl and mix.

MADE WITH LOVE!

2 Add the bicarbonate of soda and mix until it has dissolved.

3 Next, add the contact lens solution, one tablespoon at a time. Mix well and knead until your slime is ready.

4 Mix in some Valentine-themed glitter and sequins using your hands.

UNICORN GREETINGS

Want to surprise a fellow unicorn fan? Try making this cute greetings card to bring sparkle to any celebration!

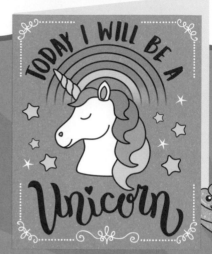

1 Ask an adult to help you cut out the page, along the vertical line.

2 Fold the card in half along the fold line.

3 Decide which lucky unicorn fan you're going to send your card to, then write their name and add your autograph.

4 Find an envelope that fits the card and write your friend's name on the envelope.

TODAY I WILL BE A *Unicorn*

Have a Magical Day!

WHOSE POOP?

Follow the lines to discover whose poop is whose!

Happy Hooves

Moonbeam

Rainbow Dancer

Buttercup

A   B   C   D

#WHOPOOPED?

♥ CRACK THE CODE

Unicorns are curious creatures that live
a charmed life! Crack the code to reveal
the magical message.

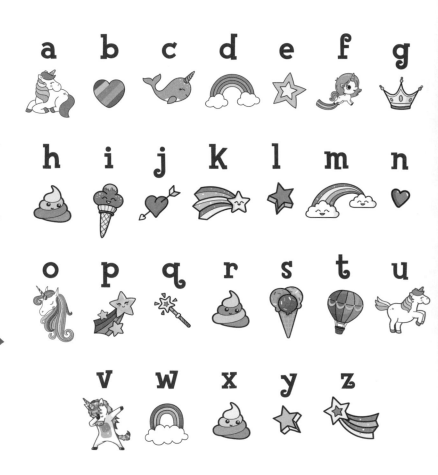

Answer is on page 93.

GORGEOUSLY GOLD SLIME

Metallic paint will give you a gorgeously gold deluxe slime – perfect for any VIP slime sessions!

What you'll need:

- 250 ml clear PVA glue
- 30 ml water
- 1/4 tsp bicarbonate of soda
- contact lens solution
- metallic acrylic paint

Tip to Try!
Add biodegradable glitter for a truly glistening slime, or try combining different coloured metallic slimes.

1

Pour the clear glue and water into a bowl and mix well.

BRING ON

2

Add the bicarbonate of soda and mix until it has dissolved, then add drops of contact lens solution and mix again.

3

Pour in a generous amount of metallic paint, then mix until the mixture begins to come away from the sides of the bowl.

4

Knead the mixture until you have a gold-standard slime consistency!

THE BLING!

WHAT'S YOUR MAGICAL NAME?

There's a little magic inside every one of us – you just have to believe! Work out your magical name below.

First, find the date on which you were born...

1 - Stunning	11 - Bedazzling	21 - Peculiar
2 - Marvellous	12 - Secretive	22 - Fiery
3 - Bewitching	13 - Fantastic	23 - Mysterious
4 - Fabulous	14 - Awesome	24 - Healing
5 - Wondrous	15 - Heavenly	25 - Charming
6 - Spellbinding	16 - Breathtaking	26 - Powerful
7 - Enchanting	17 - Mystic	28 - Astounding
8 - Charmed	18 - Extraordinary	29 - Captivating
9 - Dainty	19 - Stupendous	30 - Fascinating
10 - Curious	20 - Divine	31 - Unearthly

And now the month in which you were born...

January - Crystal	July - Rune
February - Amber	August - Harmony
March - Crescent	September - Aurora
April - Moonstone	October - Raven
May - Wanda	November - Cosmo
June - Phoenix	December - Serendipity

Write your magical name here...

POOPY SURPRISE

Colour in the shapes
with a dot to reveal
a slimy surprise!

ANSWERS

Page 9
Glitter Poop appears on pages 25, 31, 60, 69 and 82.

Page 12

Pages 18-19

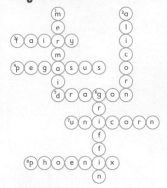

Pages 20-21

Page 33
1. UNICORN,
2. GRIFFIN,
3. MERMAID,
4. PHOENIX,
5. DRAGON,
6. ALICORN.

Page 50

Page 51
The animal is a NARWHAL.

Pages 56-57

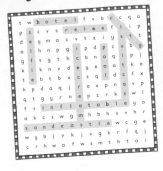

The vacay hangout is the BEACH.

Page 63
1. B, 2. F, 3. A, 4. E, 5. C, 6 D.

Page 66
Cupcakes C and H are identical.

Pages 68-69
1. H, 2. A, 3. F, 4. B, 5. E, 6. C, 7. G, 8. D.

Page 79
Unicorn 5 is the odd one out.

Page 85
1. Happy Hooves - D,
2. Rainbow Dancer - A,
3. Moonbeam - C,
4. Buttercup - B.

Pages 86-87
Leave a little sparkle wherever you go.

PICTURE CREDITS

With thanks to Abigael Longfellow, PastelSlimesUK

While every effort has been made to credit all contributors, we would like to apologize should there be any omissions or errors, and would be pleased to make any appropriate corrections for future editions of this book.

Key t – top, bottom – b, centre – c, left – l, right – r

Adobe Stock: 2–3, 14bl, 14br, 31b, 94–95, 82t, 83t, 83b Tereez; 12t, 25br, 8t, 8b, 40t, 48t, 85tcl nastazia; 26c, 26b, 27t, 27b teploeta; 30, 96bc Marina Mays; 71tl, 71tr, 63, 93br robo_s.

Cloud King Creative: 16c, 17t, 17c, 17bl, 17br, 22cr, 23t, 23tl, 23cr, 23b, 28c, 29tr, 29cl, 29br, 29cr, 36c, 37, 40b, 41, 43tl, 43tr, 46, 47, 52c, 52b, 53t, 53cl, 53cr, 58b, 59t, 59cl, 59cr, 59br, 64c, 64b, 65t, 65cl, 65cr, 72c, 72b, 73tl, 73cl, 73cr, 73br, 80br, 81t, 81t, 81c, 81bl, 81br, 88c, 89t, 89cl, 89cr, 89br.

Freepik: 39br, 60t

iStock: 1t, 1bl, 5t, 5b, 16b, 20, 21t, 22, 24t, 36bl, 37, 39tr, 44, 45, 52t, 54–55t, 67, 85, 74c Armation74; 50 fireflamenco; 38br, 39bl 3d_kot; 85, 88b, 88t Irina_Strelnikova; 62 elfiny; 79, 85 jsabirova.

Shutterstock: 1c, 5c, 65b, 86tl Riddick Patrec; 4t GraphicsRF; 1br, 24b, 56br, 64tl, 92t Daria Voskooeva; 4c, 7tl, 9t, 10b, 12cr,14cl, 15tl, 15tc, 15tr, 16t, 28tl, 28tr, 28bl, 29bl, 31, 48bl, 48br, 49, 54b, 55b, 56cl, 56bl, 57c, 59 bl, 70t, 74b, 76c, 76b, 80tl, 84, 86–87, 90t, 91cl, 91cr, 96bl, 96br Chinch; 8–9, 16–17, 22–23, 36–37, 40–41, 52–53, 58–59, 77, 78–79 Nadezda Barkova; 19tl, 72tl, 72br, 73bl Marish; 28–29 JuliJuli; 33bl, 33br, 57b, 58t, 82b Picnot; 36t, 36bl Nadezda Barkova; 43 Maria Skrigan; 46–47 PandP Studio; 51 Igdeeva Alena; 64–65, 72–73 olgdesigner; 66 Ana Angelova; 69 Inspiring; 76t Alex708; 91b twobears_art.